THE DASH DIET
FOR BEGINNERS

Lose Weight, Lower Blood Pressure,
and Improve Your Health

SUSAN ELLERBECK

ISBN-13: 978-1490320342
ISBN-10: 1490320342

Disclaimer

CONTENTS

INTRODUCTION

The United States National Institutes of Health created a special diet called the DASH Diet. This is the acronym for the far less "sexy" sounding "Dietary Approaches to Stop Hypertension".

Hypertension is the fancy way of talking about high blood pressure and the many health problems it can create. So, this diet was meant to drop the blood pressure through dietary changes rather than medications.

Does it work? Absolutely!

Additionally, what many people have since discovered is that it is not only a way of eating that is likely to help you decrease your blood pressure and risk of heart attack, but also a diet that helps:

- **Reduce "bad" cholesterol**
- **Improve insulin sensitivity**
- **Lose weight**
- **Prevent kidney stones**
- **Decrease risk of certain cancers**
- **Cut stroke risk**

Okay, you might think, it is obviously a very wise way to eat...so, what's it all about?

That is the focus of this book! In the following chapters we'll take a long look at the main components of the DASH diet - food - and learn how you really "are what you eat". So, if you are ready to control a long list of health concerns by making good dietary choices, let's begin!

DEFINING THE DASH DIET

A Basic Definition of DASH

To keep it as simple as possible, the DASH diet is "research based" and uses a lot of fruits and vegetables, nonfat or low fat dairy products, whole gains, nuts and beans, and a bit of lean meat, poultry or fish.

What does research based actually mean? Let's take a quick look at the history behind DASH to find out.

The Research on DASH

The DASH diet is the result of a study "conducted at five academic medical centers in the United States," which used three different dietary patterns. It was proposed by the National Institutes of Health and the National Heart, Lung and Blood Institute, and was conducted by John Hopkins University, Duke University Medical Center, Kaiser Permanente in Portland, Oregon, Brigham and Women's Hospital, and Pennington Biomedical Research Center.

The three dietary patterns that study used were the "typical American diet", the "typical American diet, but higher in fruits and vegetables", and the DASH diet. Though all three groups were allowed to consume roughly 3k mg of sodium every day (which is about 1.25 teaspoons of straight table salt), it was only DASH that provided large quantities of minerals and nutrients.

Results of the First Studies

What happened during the studies? The "typical American diet, but with more fruits and vegetables", and the DASH diet both saw reduced blood pressure, but it was DASH that had the largest number of benefits for those already displaying signs of hypertension, or being diagnosed with it.

Essentially, the study proved diets relying mostly on fruits, vegetables, and low fat dairy products were the best for controlling blood pressure.

This led to a follow up study that sought to use the optimal DASH diet plus reduced sodium as well.

The Second Study

The second study did also relied on randomly assigned diets, but this time it was the "typical American diet" versus the DASH diet. Also, the group of participants was divided into three sodium intake groups - high sodium of 3300mg, moderate sodium of 2400mg, and low sodium of 1500mg.

Again, the results were remarkable with those on DASH and lower sodium plans reducing their blood pressure by very measurable amounts. In fact, when the 1500mg plan was used along with DASH diet and a few lifestyle changes (such as adding 30 minutes of daily exercise) the participants experienced an average blood pressure reduction of 8.9/4.5 mm Hg (systolic/diastolic).

Would such small amounts matter? Of course, and we should take a moment to talk about blood pressure and sodium to ensure you understand the value of the changes that can occur when DASH and a low sodium diet are used.

A LOOK AT BLOOD PRESSURE

Blood pressure is measured in two ways - systolic and diastolic. It is meant to gauge the force exerted by the blood moving through the arteries. With each beat of your heart the blood is moved through the body, but it isn't just one evenly sized channel through which blood must flow. There are the arteries that taper into capillaries (tiny blood vessels), and it is here that essential nutrients and oxygen are sent into your organs and tissue.

Thus, blood flow and circulation are essential. The circulation also moves other fluids such as lymph from the capillaries and back into the veins where blood returns to the heart and oxygenates the lungs. There is a lot going on, and the pressure in the system is pretty important.

Clearly, it is best when the vessels are healthy and allow the blood to move easily. This reduces pressure on the heart and transfers nutrients and oxygen efficiently. When the arteries are stiff and narrow, on the other hand, the pressure on the heart increases and there are risks to arteries that have too much pressure built up inside of them.

So, we measure blood pressure in those two ways mentioned. The systolic pressure is a measurement of the pressure inside of the veins when the heart is pumping or moving blood, and the diastolic is the pressure in the arteries in the "rest" between heart beats.

Blood pressure readings look like this:

systolic/diastolic Hg

The Hg stands for the chemical element "Mercury". The device that is used to measure your blood pressure (known as a sphygmomanometer - say THAT five times fast!) relies on a Mercury filled meter that the physician or nurse reads. They put the cuff on the arm and inflate it to increase the "volume" of the sound the blood makes as it passes through the arteries. They will then place a stethoscope on an artery while looking at the Mercury filled gauge. As soon as they hear sound they make their first reading.

So, on that first "whoosh" they know it is the blood beating through the arteries, and that is the number they use for systolic pressure. They wait for all sound to fade and take the diastolic reading. The readings taken from the Mercury filled tube connected to the cuff are read in millimeter increments. Thus, your blood pressure reads as systolic/diastolic Hg (or mm Hg).

What is a healthy blood pressure? Medical experts seem to constantly change their thoughts on this matter, but currently, the optimal measure is 120/80 Hg. Naturally, this figure varies for different people and what one person experiences as low blood pressure could be normal for another. Generally speaking, when the systolic is more than 140 and the diastolic over 90, the person is hypertensive or has high blood pressure.

Of course, the higher blood pressure reading has to be constant and when the person is in a restive state. Blood pressure does increase or decrease all of the time and can be affected by:

- Drinking caffeine;
- Having a full bladder;
- Smoking on a constant basis; and
- Physical activity.

For example, a healthy person who swallows a glass of cola and runs a lap around a track will naturally have higher blood pressure than when they are just sitting on the sofa.

Additionally, we know that dietary choices can create chronic blood pressure problems too. This takes us back to sodium and the DASH diet.

Excess Sodium and What it Does to the Body

Sodium is what makes you "retain" fluid throughout the body. This extra fluid forces the heart to work harder if it is to do its job of moving blood through the many vessels that carry it. This means that excess fluid puts pressure on the arteries, and this can (according to the American Heart Association) lead to:

- Fluid in the lungs
- Problems with coronary arteries
- Loss of vision
- Peripheral artery disease

- Stroke

- Kidney damage

- ED

- Memory loss

- Angina

The good news, as you have already started to learn, is that following the DASH diet and taking in the lower sodium levels will combine to lower blood pressure substantially and help with many other issues as well.

Though we already quoted the DASH studies as showing an average reduction of 8.9/4.5 mm Hg, those with confirmed hypertension experienced an average reduction of 11.5/5.7 mm Hg. This is amazing! For instance, someone who had a resting blood pressure of around 150/85 might be able to drop their numbers to 140/79 (a healthy blood pressure) by diet alone!

DASH DIET BENEFITS

The four agencies doing the studies concluded that their studies did have an impact on high blood pressure. They also determined that following the DASH plan and lowering sodium would always result in a lower blood pressure, but it was also determined that further studies would be necessary to determine if DASH eating reduced the risk of many common chronic diseases like cancer, heart disease, osteoporosis, etc.

Generally, however, they did determine and report that everyone can benefit from following DASH and not only patients with high blood pressure.

DASH can help everyone? How can reducing sodium and using diet to control blood pressure be of benefit to those without any issues related to hypertension or blood pressure? Kids, healthy teens, and active adults can benefit from reduced sodium?

We know that any reduction in blood pressure is going to help reduce subsequent health risks, but how does DASH combat things like cancer? It has to do with the increased consumption of whole grains and fruits and vegetables. These boost fiber intake, and nutrient levels in conjunction with lowering the sodium. The increase in nutrients, vitamins, and fiber are truly good for everyone.

The Other Benefits of DASH

Though designed to help people reduce sodium (salt) intake, and to naturally reduce blood pressure, DASH also works wonders for weight loss, chronic disease, and more. Thus, you can use the information we provide to you about DASH to accomplish more than one goal.

For example, in "diet speak", the DASH diet is a high fiber and low to moderate fat diet. It keeps your daily intake of sodium to absolutely minimal levels (up to up to 2,300 milligrams daily) and also cuts most of the unhealthy cholesterols and fats.

In addition to helping with health problems by cutting unhealthy food content, it also boosts the nutrient content of the diet too. Those who follow it closely find that they consume a lot of beneficial nutrients like:

- Potassium

- Calcium

- Magnesium

Many people can benefit from following this sort of eating plan, and it is a diet that is safe for everyone - meaning it is a good way for the entire family to eat. It doesn't limit calories to dramatically low levels (with options for 1600, 2000, and 2600 calories per day) and provides very clear guidelines for the appropriate balance of food sources.

For instance, consider the following list of foods to eat using the DASH diet and how many servings could be consumed. The servings indicated are for 1600 to 2600 calorie daily diets and some foods are tagged as "per week" because they do have higher fat content.

- Grains (should be whole grains) - 6-12 per day
- Fruits - 4-6 per day
- Vegetables - 4-6 per day
- Low fat or non fat dairy - 2-4 per day
- Lean meats, fish, poultry - 1.5 to 2.5 per day
- Nuts, seeds, and legumes - 3-6 per week
- Fat and sugar - 2-4

That is really all there is to it, but you will need to learn about "action plans", which are more than just discovering how mix and match foods. That is what the remainder of this book is all about.

In the next sections we will give you actionable steps, complete explanations, and even meal plans that really help you to maximize the way you can put the DASH diet to work for you, or your whole family.

WHAT YOU CAN EXPECT

Before we start looking at the way to actually "do" DASH eating, we should point out a few final factors about this diet.

1. It IS a diet, but NOT one designed specifically for weight loss. It is meant to supply someone with approximately two thousand calories per day, but this may be too high for your particular needs. A bit later we will review how to discover your suggested daily caloric intake, and how to use that to help with weight loss. For now, you need to know that DASH is not primarily a calorie reduced diet.

2. It is a DIET and that means that it requires you to change your way of eating, your way of viewing food, and altering the choices you might normally make. For example, many people find the daily fruits and vegetable amounts a bit of a challenge because the average American gets 2 - 3 servings of fruits and vegetables combined each day and that is barely half of what DASH requires. So, you need to understand that it requires you to commit to major changes in the way you eat each day, and that it takes very focused efforts for the first few weeks.

3. It can reduce the blood pressure by up to fourteen points in as little as a few weeks time. This means you do need to work with a physician to monitor your condition if you are using the diet for blood pressure reduction and/or control.

4. The goal of this scientifically designed diet is to reduce sodium intake to two levels - moderately or extremely. The "standard "DASH diet allows 2300mg of sodium each day while the "lower" DASH diet allows for only 1500mg. The average person tends to ingest around 3500mg of sodium each day and that is what can easily lead to higher blood pressure. DASH drops the levels by relying on specific foods and on foods that also help to reduce sodium, boost your nutrient levels, and generally create optimal nutrition.

5. This diet allows you to eat red meats, small amounts of fat, and even some sweets from time to time. It is unique in this way, and is much more workable over the long term than other "diets". This means it is more of a plan for healthy life rather than a temporary way of eating meant to create some temporary and hard to maintain results.

6. Remember too that it is always a good plan to consider the best quality foods when following a diet as fruit and vegetable heavy as this one. Go for organic when possible, and always try to consider the whole grain versions of everything from bread and crackers to pastas.

Now that you have a basic understanding of the DASH diet, let's look at the details you need to know in order to take your first steps into the DASH diet.

PLANNING YOUR DASH

Now comes the time when you can begin to make your plans for using the DASH diet to meet your own personal goals. The biggest first step is to understand precisely what those goals might be.

For example, people who use the DASH diet might be:

- Attempting to control blood pressure through diet rather than medication;

- Seeking to transition themselves (and their family) into a healthier way of life;

- Trying to lose weight;

- Hoping to develop a plan for eating that is simple and which can be used throughout life instead of temporarily to address a health issue; or

- All of these things.

So, ask yourself why you are exploring the DASH diet and if you can get more than just a single result from your efforts. This matters because we are going to encourage you to make plans and track results to prove to yourself that your hard work is really paying off.

Consider that you might be doing the DASH diet only to control blood pressure. If that is the case, you need to begin finding ways to measure the blood pressure on a fairly regular basis, keep track of the figures, and talk with a physician to be sure you are remaining healthy.

Are You Trying to Lose Weight or Manage Blood Pressure?

That is the most common question that many people ask themselves. While there are all kinds of insurance tables and expert opinions about weight, it is really a matter of your personal opinion. You could be a very large framed person of average height and read that your weight falls into an "overweight" category, but that might be incredibly inaccurate. The same applies for the small framed person with a petite build who reads that they are underweight when they are, in fact, extremely healthy.

So, the best way to understand if you are in a healthy weight range is to speak directly with your physician. They will measure body weight, height, the amount of body fat you carry, and any other factors that indicate whether you should drop weight, gain weight, or maintain your current weight.

The good news is that the DASH diet can meet all three needs because it can be designed to accommodate calorie counts as well as sodium intake levels!

After asking a physician for an opinion about your weight, it's time to discover the number of calories needed to maintain your current weight. This is known as the Basal Metabolic Rate, or the BMR.

The BMR

The BMR is basically the amount of energy required to allow your body to function "at rest". This means that the BMR measures the number of calories you NEED each day to maintain your current weight, and also figures this number based on ZERO energy expenditure. In other words - your BMR is the number of calories you could eat during a single day if all you did was lie on the couch.

Interestingly enough, however, you use around 60 to 70 percent of your daily calories in this way-just functioning without activity. You also burn around 10% of the calories you use when digesting as well. Yes, you can calculate ten percent of the daily calorie intake and subtract it because your body uses energy to extract energy!

How do you know your BMR? Use the "Harris Benedict" formulas below:

Adult female: 655 + (4.3 x weight in lbs.) + (4.7 x height in inches) - (4.7 x age in years); or

Adult male: 66 + (6.3 x body weight in lbs.) + (12.9 x height in inches) - (6.8 x age in years).

Here is an example of a 42 year old woman who stands 5'7" and weighs 145 pounds.

655 + 623.5 + 314.9 - 197.4 = 1396 calories per day and fully at rest.

When you have that number you also know the type of diet you must consume each day if you are trying to lose weight, gain weight, or simply maintain your weight. Now, before you argue that the woman described above would have to seriously restrict calorie intake to drop weight, remember that the figure is for a body at total rest.

If you add 30 minutes of activity each day, you also alter the number of calories that have to be consumed to maintain the weight as well. For example, if that woman took a brisk 45 minute walk each day, did regular house chores, and played with her kids for an hour, it would bump up the number of calories she could consume without gaining weight.

Take a few moments to calculate your BMR and jot it down. Then consider what your goals might be: lose weight, gain weight, or maintain current weight.

- If you are seeking to lose weight you should try to lose no more than two pounds each week - which is seven thousand calories subtracted from the diet! To do this would mean to create a daily deficit in the BMR.

  The woman described above would have to monitor food intake, track calories, and really boost her activity level tremendously to drop that much weight in a single week.

Thus, it is best to lose weight in increments like half of a pound to a pound per week.

- To gain weight is just the reverse. The dieter would choose a higher calorie eating plan and do only enough exercise for health rather than for calorie burning. In other words, they could use the 2000 or 2600 calorie eating plan and do around 30 minutes to an hour of exercise each day and slowly gain weight.

- The person seeking to maintain their weight need only calculate the BMR and use an eating plan and exercise regimen that kept their daily calories at the BMR amount determined.

After you understand caloric needs, it is much easier to begin using DASH for your chosen goals.

No matter what you do, the DASH diet is going to drop your sodium intake, which tends to release fluid held in the body - often called "water weight" - and that can feel like weight loss. If you stick with the diet, that water weight will stay away too!

Of course, the DASH plan is remarkably helpful in this way because it is richer in potassium than many other diets. This is a natural compound that is great for keeping blood pressure at health levels. The National Institutes for Health reported that a potassium rich diet did reduce higher blood pressures, but also insisted that it was food sources and not supplements that generated the best results.

They recommended that fish, dairy, and fruits and vegetables be put to use as the primary sources because of their bioavailable potassium that helped with bone loss and other issues.

So, not only is reducing the sodium in your diet part of the DASH plan, but adding nutrients that also help to regulate blood pressure and metabolism is as well.

GETTING STARTED WITH DASH

How exactly does one begin "doing" the DASH diet? It is all a matter of tracking the foods eaten and making sure to stay within the established guidelines. You are going to have to choose if you are going for the standard sodium level of 2300mg or if you are doing it for optimal reduction in the blood pressure and consuming no more than 1500 mg per day.

Either way, the DASH eating plan looks like this:

- Total fat: 27% of calories

- Saturated fat: 6% of calories

- Protein: 18% of calories

- Carbohydrate: 55% of calories

- Fiber: 30 g

- Cholesterol: 150 mg

- Sodium: 1,500 to 2,300 mg

- Potassium: 4,700 mg

- Calcium: 1,250 mg

- Magnesium: 500 mg

As you can see, the diet is very heart healthy and limits cholesterol and saturated fats to minimal amounts. The boost in nutrients, protein, and fiber are also extremely healthy, but it is the sodium where the biggest returns can be found.

Some Words on Sodium

The DASH diet tries to avoid heavy use of low sodium or specialty products. Instead, it asks you to remember that your food choices are what impact your results and success levels the most. In fact, the NIH emphasized that only a small amount of the sodium consumed each day comes from a salt shaker on the table. Instead, they report that it is processed food that is to blame for the SAD's high sodium intake.

They recommend label reading and the purchase of "low sodium" labeled foods as some of the best ways to control this hidden sodium intake. For example, baked goods, seasonings, soy sauces, and even some OTC antacids are extremely high in dietary sodium according to their reports.

It helps to visualize your daily limits in order to understand how your choices play such a dramatic role in the outcome. Those using the 2,300 mg plan should imagine a teaspoon measure of table salt as their daily "cap". Those on the heavily restricted sodium plans, the 1,500 mg diets, should imagine 2/3 of a teaspoon as their daily limit.

That is not a lot at all, but many restaurant and pre-packaged foods have far more than these daily limits. Consider this list of common DASH foods and the amount of sodium they contain:

- Low fat and fat free dairy products
  - Milk, 1 cup: 107mg
  - Yogurt, 1 cup: 175mg
  - Cheese, 1.5 ounces: up to 450 mg
- Whole grain products
  - Cooked rice, pasta, or cereal, 1/2 cup: 5mg
  - Bread, 1 slice: 175mg
- Lean meats
  - Canned tuna, 3 ounces: 350mg
  - Fresh meat, poultry or fish, 3 ounces: 90mg

You could eat a large amount of these healthy foods without worrying greatly about the sodium content. If, on the other hand, you opted for a slice of roasted ham (1020mg), a glass of tomato juice (330mg), and a 1/2 of canned beans (400mg), you could easily exceed your daily amounts quickly.

Thus, the DASH dieter has to start thinking in terms of "whole foods" rather than any sort of processed, pre-cooked, or pre-packaged foods, and has to transition themselves into a diet that is flavored with herbs and citrus rather than salt and bottled sauces.

Let's take a look at using DASH to reduce blood pressure by also considering the amount of sodium.

DASH FOR BLOOD PRESSURE

So, if you are going to do the DASH diet as a way of reducing your blood pressure without having to rely on medications, the following steps are necessary:

1. Calculate the BMR
2. Use a DASH planner (supplied in the last chapter) to begin formulating your daily meals
3. Choose a safe amount of daily exercise, and determine how that impacts the daily caloric intake
4. Determine which sodium reduction techniques will help you the most (the list appears below)
5. Begin by adding one DASH meal per day until you are completely transitioned into the diet.

Our Top Sodium Reduction Techniques

It is not easy to go from a salty diet (common in the United States and other parts of the world) to one that is flavored mostly by natural ingredients rather than actual salt or sodium. To help with this we provide the following tips and techniques:

1. Become a perimeter shopper - most grocery stores keep the whole foods on the perimeter of the store. The produce, dairy, fresh meats and fish, and even "bulk" grains are usually outside of the aisles.

2. Avoid canned vegetables, fruits, and foods. Instead, opt for fresh or frozen choices and double check their labels for added sodium.

3. When purchasing condiments such as ketchup, soy sauce, broth, or other pre-package foods, always go for the "low sodium" or even the "no sodium added" varieties. Double check the labels to ensure that nothing else has been added that could be unhealthy.

4. Don't buy "cured" meats or "smoked" foods. Bacon, pickles, olives, barbecue sauces, teriyaki sauce, etc. are always high in sodium - even if their labels proclaim them to be lower sodium versions. If you do use the low sodium condiments, limit them to very small amounts and be sure to keep track of the amount of sodium each serving delivers.

5. Don't salt any cooking waters or fluids. We often forget that salting the pasta water, rice, or even the hot breakfast cereal will tip the scales in terms of our sodium consumption for the day.

6. Avoid frozen dinners, convenience foods, dressings, takeout food like pizza because these tend to have enormous amounts of sodium.

7. If you do use a food that is canned and labeled as low sodium (you won't use any other type of canned food!), be sure that you still rinse it off before using it. Whether this is canned veggies or meats, it is good to rinse away as much of the sodium as possible.

8. Learn all about spices. Many people discover that they prefer the flavors that come from herbs, spices, citrus, and sodium and salt free spice blends that can be used to give almost any sort of cuisine a real "kick" in flavor.

With these tactics for getting started with DASH for blood pressure, you should be able to see measurable results in a matter of weeks.

DASH FOR WEIGHT LOSS

1. Calculate the BMR and determine the number needed to create an appropriate weekly deficit (i.e. -3500 calories each week will translate to a full pound of weight lost)

2. Use a DASH planner to begin formulating your daily meals

3. Choose a safe amount of daily exercise, and determine how that impacts the daily caloric intake and the resulting loss of weight.

4. Determine which activity boosting techniques will help you the most (the list appears below)

5. Begin by adding one DASH meal per day until you are completely transitioned into the diet.

Now, #5 tells you to transition into the diet, but this is not as simple as that sounds. Why not? You are trying to lose weight, and that means cutting calories. It is not so easy to understand just how to do this, and so here are our techniques for eliminating calories easily while using DASH.

Tactics for Lowering Calorie Intake

1. Increase vegetables - don't broil a chicken breast and serve with a side of veggies when you can stretch that chicken by using it in a stir fry that is mostly vegetables and herbs. The same goes for a lean beef burger - skip fries and a small veggie side when you can cut the meat in half and fill the burger with diced vegetables before broiling it! Try to find ways to fill up on vegetables and keep calories lower than ever.

2. Increase fruits - skip the carbohydrate heavy snacks like crackers (which are often full of sodium anyway) and substitute with a piece of fruit. Use a small amount of dried fruit if you are feeling a lag in energy. Also, stir fresh fruit into yogurt, cereal, and fat free ice cream to boost flavor and add more fruits to the diet. Fruit is an ideal snack, but you can always find ways to use it as an ingredient in meals.

3. Use no-fat dairy if possible as this cuts calories by substantial numbers. For example, a regular scoop of ice cream versus the fat free stuff is going to mean more than one hundred calories saved!

4. Buy "low fat" everything. If you are buying condiments, dairy foods, butter/margarine, and cereals, try to always choose the no or low fat varieties as these are usually much lower in total calorie counts.

5. Watch the serving sizes! So often we don't actually measure the foods we eat. When a list of suggested foods says "three ounces of meat" be sure that is what you are eating, etc.

6. Become a stringent label reader. We don't always read food labeling and this can lead to shocking results. High sodium, fat, cholesterol, and chemical additives are often the end result of skipping the label reading.

7. When buying canned fruits, go for those in their own juices or in water. Skip the sugary sweetened fruits that are full of empty calories.

8. If you have to have the "crunch", go for air popped popcorn or a few carrot sticks instead of chips or rice cakes as these are always full of fat and sodium.

9. Stop drinking soda and carbonated beverages. They are full of calories and sodium. Stick to water with lemon or lime.

Our Top Fitness Techniques

The recommended level of daily exercise is a mere 30 minutes, and it doesn't even have to be all at once. Ten minutes of brisk walking at lunch, twenty minutes of active play with the kids or the family pet, and ten minutes of weight training can boost your health substantially - and burn the calories needed to shed weight.

We also recommend:

1. Incorporate your daily exercise into your DASH planner. This ensures you create a schedule that you can stick to.

2. Find an exercise buddy. Whether for accountability (who else do you answer to when you skip daily exercise?), safety, companionship, or competition, workout buddies are known to help anyone achieve exercise and fitness goals.

3. Try some Cross Fit or Cross Training. This means alternating between a range of cardio, strength, and stretching to get optimal results. There are many good books and websites that can show even a novice how to get going.

4. Write down goals and keep track of when you reach them. Without a "road map" for success, you won't know where you are going and having a formal list of goals tends to keep people "honest".

5. Schedule some down time. Any fitness expert would agree that a day off once each week is a great way to keep motivated and get the best results with exercise.

6. Reward your success. Once each month you should make a point of assessing your progress and giving yourself a reward for a job well done. Something like an MP3 file for each pound lost, a new cookbook, or some new clothing are all great ideas.

DASH FOR BOTH WEIGHT LOSS AND BLOOD PRESSURE

We consider this approach on its own because it does require some special considerations.

For example, even a weight loss of three to five pounds can have an effect on blood pressure. If you are already diagnosed as hypertensive, and using some medications, the combination of exercise, the DASH diet, and its immediate results could result in problems.

The medication may actually "overdo" things, and so the best way to use DASH for both weight loss and blood pressure is to consult with your doctor first and discuss the safest way to change your eating and your way of life. They may want you to make some visits as you transition into the DASH plan and just have weight, blood pressure, and general health checked for stability and safety.

Now you have the most basic principles, and that means it is time to take a good look at the actual DASH diet components - food!

THE FOOD GROUPS ON DASH

Perhaps you are someone who eats according to the food pyramids, or the newer version known as the food plate? If so, you already understand how foods are divided into very clear "groups". DASH also uses food groups, and keeps extremely specific track of the foods you should be eating each day, and precisely how much of them you should include for the best results.

In the last section of this book we provide you with very clear tables of eating plans based on caloric needs. There are tables for 1,600, 2,000, and 2,600 calories each day. In them are the numbers of servings of each food group, and an explanation or sample of a single serving as well. This is to help you to make the most effective choices for your own DASH diet efforts.

Again, we need to emphasize that the quality of the foods you choose will have a direct correlation to your results. Go for whole foods, organic when possible, always fresh over frozen, and if you must buy in cans just be sure to rinse as much as possible to eliminate the sodium.

A Closer Look at the Food Groups

Let's take a look at these groups now in order to understand what they are and why they are included in DASH. They are the "bread and butter" and "meat and bones" of the diet, which is ironic because such ingredients only scarcely appear in the lists! Instead, you have a diet rich in nutrients and low in fat and which is built upon:

- Grains (6 to 8 servings a day) - whole grains are really the way to go and these would provide you with a huge amount of fiber and energy (since they will be the main sources of carbohydrates in the daily diet. Choose "brown" over "white" (such as brown rice over white rice, or brown breads over white breads) but do read the labels to be sure they are 100% whole grain or whole wheat, etc.

- Vegetables (4 to 5 servings a day) - you will see that the famous "rainbow on your plate" concept can apply to vegetables as well as fruits when following the DASH diet. Red tomatoes, orange yams and carrots, brilliant green broccoli and spinach, and everything else that is full of nutrients, minerals, vitamins and fiber. Remember that vegetables are not just a side dish to a slab of protein or pile of grains. They can be the main course on their own. Remember too that many frozen vegetables are just as nutritious (and sometimes even more so) than their fresh cousins.

- Fruits (4 to 5 servings a day) - ready to eat snacks, fruit is always any diet's saving grace. Loaded with the same high amounts of fiber, nutrients, and vitamins as vegetables, they are also low in fat and easy to digest. You can use them as individual snacks or as boosters to other foods like yogurt or even salad. Remember to leave fruits with peels when possible as this adds to the fiber level and even gives new textures to recipes. Remember too that you can rely on citrus as a good salt substitute, but be careful about drug interactions as grapefruit and other citrus are known for negative reactions with some medicine.

- Dairy (2 to 3 servings a day) - as a primary source for calcium, foods like yogurt, cheese, and milk should not be eliminated. Just try to obtain the low fat and fat free versions when possible. Keep in mind that 27% of calories can come from fat, and a single cup of Greek yogurt can often have that same amount (or more) of the daily fat intake! Dairy is going to also be a good source of dessert substitutes, so try to save some space when you are feeling the urge to splurge on the diet.

- Lean meat, poultry and fish (6 or fewer servings a day) - you will get a lot of your B vitamins, iron, and zinc from this food group, as well as protein. Don't, however, keep meat as the center of a meal. This is because it can contain a lot of cholesterol and fat, as well as sodium if it is prepared or processed. Other ways to enhance the meats you choose is to cut off any remaining fats, broil or roast meats (rather than frying), and try to add the fish that are Omega-3 rich, such as salmon or tuna, to the weekly diet.

- Nuts, seeds and legumes (4 to 5 servings a week) - excellent sources of potassium and magnesium as well as protein, this food group is also very fiber rich too. They are also, unfortunately, calorie dense foods and should be eaten only to the amounts recommended. The fats that they do contain, however, are the "healthy" kinds (as is the fat in avocados). Many people on DASH also eventually shift to the use of tofu and soybean proteins because they are so nutrient rich and have the same levels of protein as meat. Consider this as you get deeper into your DASH eating plans.

- Fats and oils (2 to 3 servings a day) - this is a sore subject for some because they don't really understand the issue. Firstly, you need fat in the diet in order to allow the body to absorb vitamins and build the immune system. Obviously, too much fat is going to be unhealthy, as is too much of the "bad fat". So, those on the DASH plan have to get less than 30% of their daily calories from fat, and need to focus on the unsaturated or monounsaturated types. Avoid the saturated fats as much as possible - such as those found in butter, eggs, whole milk, shortening, and certain meats. Also read food labels to gauge how much daily fat and saturated fat a single serving of any food supplies.

- Sweets (5 or fewer a week) - isn't it good news that your DASH diet can include some sweets each week? You can use a range of treats to fulfill this part of the plan, including plain table sugar, hard candies, some gummy candies, and even a sweetened beverage like lemonade.

- Alcohol - there is no call for alcohol in the DASH diet plan, but you are allowed one drink per day on the plan. Be aware, however, that alcohol consumption does increase the blood pressure.

- Caffeine - found in coffee, tea, energy drinks, and other foods or beverages, it is not disallowed from the DASH plan, but it is something to consider. A single cup of coffee can impact the blood pressure in a negative way, and that means that frequent caffeine consumption may be adding to a person's problems.

Using the Details

Now that you understand the essential foods you will have to use, and how many servings you can consume in a day, it is time to get started. You will be surprised at how easy it can be to eat according to DASH guidelines, but many people still feel a bit confused.

Because of that we suggest that you start by tracking your "typical" food choices for a few days or a full week before getting started with DASH. In this way you can see where you need to make changes and where you may already fall into the guidelines (i.e. you eat 2.5 servings of fruit already, etc.)

Remember too that the DASH plan is adaptable for people of all ages, and even of all dietary styles. For instance, dedicated vegetarians will find it easy to follow DASH, but so too will the committed carnivores of the world as well.

You don't have to invest in special gear, supplements (in fact, supplements are frowned on because they are not as beneficial as food sources), powders and drinks, or other paraphernalia to succeed. All you need to do is develop a plan, stick to it, track your results, and feel elation over your success!

SAMPLE MENUS FOR THE DASH DIET

Up until this point we haven't yet explained that the DASH diet follows that common suggestion of eating at least three meals each day as well as a few snacks. So, that means that all plans are going to include:

- Breakfast
- Lunch
- Dinner
- Snacks

You can decide if your "snack" is a dessert after a meal or something that you enjoy at a time during the day when you might need a boost in energy.

The Rules of Averages

Also, we want to talk about "averages". For instance, on a typical day you might find you eat three servings of fruit and fall well under the sodium level. That would mean you exceeded one area and remained below the target on another. The next day may find you eating one serving of fruit and exceeding sodium by a few milligrams.

Does this mean you are doing DASH wrong? No. Try to keep in mind that the diet is meant to be healthy and to maintain the blood pressure through dietary choices. This means you are shooting for weekly averages as well as daily averages.

That does not imply that you can enjoy a sodium "free for all" one day and cut it out for the next two days. It is always going to be a case of "moderation in all things" but don't go overboard with too much regulation. This is because you do sincerely want the DASH way of eating to become a way of life that is easy to maintain. If you are struggling and feeling anxious all of the time about the way you are eating it is not something you will do forever.

If, on the other hand, you know that the handful of popcorn at the movies is okay because you will be vigilant about sodium the rest of the day, well...it does seem far more likely that you'll stick with it.

The best way to understand and master DASH eating is to begin by drafting your plans. We give you basic planners in the last section, but for now we will show you a few sample days of eating DASH-style in order to demonstrate how simple it will be.

A Typical 1600 Calorie Day

Breakfast

- 1 whole-wheat bagel
- 2 tablespoons of sodium free peanut butter
- 1 medium banana
- 1 cup fat-free milk

Lunch

- 2 slices whole-wheat bread
- 1 teaspoon sodium free mustard
- 1 tablespoon low-fat mayonnaise
- 2 ounces roasted turkey
- Sliced tomato and lettuce
- ½ cup baby carrots
- 1 cup fat-free milk

Dinner

- 1 baked chicken breast (3 ounces)
- 1 cup brown rice
- ½ cup steamed green beans
- 1 cup romaine lettuce
- ½ cup tomato wedges
- 2 tablespoons low sodium and low-fat salad dressing
- Herbal tea

Snacks

- 1 cup low fat or fat-free yogurt
- 1 cup fresh seasonal fruit
- 1 medium apple

A 2000 calorie day would be the same, except the sandwich could have three full ounces of turkey and the snacks could include an additional cup of seasonal fruit and a cup of sliced cucumbers.

A 2600 calorie day would follow the same plan, but breakfast would include a one ounce serving of whole grain bran cereal and four ounces of orange juice. Lunch would have the same 3 ounce serving of turkey as the 2k plan, but an additional 1 ounce of crackers could be added. Dinner could include a small whole grain roll, and the snacks could also include 1/2 cup of frozen berries and 1/4 cup of whole grain granola in addition to the snacks for the 2k day.

Sodium Levels and Eating Plans

What about an example of diets with specific sodium levels? After all, the DASH diet is not strictly about calories but more about the sodium. Let's take a look at a 2,000 calorie day with the two approaches to sodium. We'll view the 2,300 mg sodium day first, and then look at the things altered to lower the sodium to 1,500 mg.

2,000 Calorie Day with 2,300 mg of Sodium

Breakfast

- 3/4 cup bran cereal

- 1 medium banana

- 1 cup low fat milk

- 1 slice whole wheat bread

- 1 tsp. margarine

- 1 cup orange juice

Lunch

- 2 ounces baked chicken

- 2 slices whole wheat bread

- 1 tablespoon low sodium Dijon mustard

- 1/2 cucumber slices

- 1/2 cup tomato wedges

- 1 tablespoon seeds

- 1 teaspoon low sodium dressing

- 1/2 cup seasonal fruit

Dinner

- 3 ounces beef

- 2 tablespoon fat free/sodium free gravy

- 1 cup green beans

- 1 small potato

- 1 tablespoon fat free sour cream

- 1 tablespoon low fat cheddar

- 1 tablespoon scallions

- 1 small whole wheat roll

- 1 teaspoon margarine

- 1 small apple

- 1 cup low fat milk

- Snacks

- 1/3 cup almonds

- 1/4 cup raisins

- 1/2 cup fat free yogurt

The same 2,000 eating plan for the 1,500mg sodium DASH dieter would look like this:

Breakfast

- 3/4 cup bran cereal - REPLACED with 3/4 of shredded wheat

- 1 medium banana

- 1 cup low fat milk

- 1 slice whole wheat bread

- 1 teaspoon margarine - REPLACED with 1 teaspoon unsalted margarine

- 1 cup orange juice

Lunch

- 2 ounces baked chicken

- 2 slices whole wheat bread

- 1 tablespoon low sodium Dijon mustard - REPLACED with regular no-salt mustard

- 1/2 cucumber slices

- 1/2 cup tomato wedges

- 1 tablespoon seeds

- 1 teaspoon low sodium dressing

- 1/2 cup seasonal fruit

Dinner

- 3 ounces beef

- 2 tablespoon fat free/sodium free gravy

- 1 cup green beans

- 1 small potato

- 1 tablespoon fat free sour cream

- 1 tablespoon low fat cheddar- REPLACED with reduced fat, low sodium cheddar

- 1 tablespoon scallions

- 1 small whole wheat roll

- 1 teaspoon margarine- REPLACED with unsalted margarine

- 1 small apple

- 1 cup low fat milk

Snacks

- 1/3 cup almonds
- 1/4 cup raisins
- 1/2 cup fat free yogurt

You can see that the changes are tiny, which shows how important it will become to start tracking sodium. Just a few pats of margarine, a dab of mustard, and the wrong choice in breakfast cereals can make a big difference in your results.

Now that you have some good examples, we can start "putting it all together", which is the topic of the next chapter.

THE DASH CHECKLIST

Up to this point you have:

1. Determined why you will do the change - i.e. to drop the blood pressure, lose a bit of weight, shift to a healthier way of life, etc.

2. Established goals and written them down.

3. Met with your doctor to get an accurate blood pressure and to talk about your plans and goals. And then made plans to follow up with them if necessary.

4. Determined your BMR.

5. Identified how to use the BMR to help you meet your goals - i.e. you know if you should use the 1,600; 2,000; or the 2,600 calorie plans.

6. Have tracked your typical eating patterns for two days or more.

7. Have reviewed the foods that are part of the DASH plan and stocked your pantry and refrigerator (using the shopping list at the end of this book) with the foods that you can eat. (You might also want to "purge" the home of foods that might

tempt you to go off track. Unopened items can be donated to a local food pantry and opened foods can be offered to friends, neighbors, family, etc. You might even have a "Going Healthy" dinner party and use up the foods that you won't be eating very often in the future!)

8. Found a workout buddy to help you stick to your intended exercise plans.

9. Have started to read labels in order to understand what daily amounts are found in the packaged or prepared foods that you do choose.

10. Have used the basic planner to begin adding DASH eating to your daily diet.

11. Have chosen a date by which you will have transitioned entirely into DASH.

MAKING THE CHANGE TO DASH

Now, why can't you just jump right into it? You absolutely can, but we do need to remind you of a few things:

- The increase in fiber in the DASH plan can often be a bit of a shock to the system for those unaccustomed to it. This can leave people feeling bloated, gassy, and even experiencing digestive trouble. Rather than flinging yourself into the DASH diet, you may want to begin with one or two meals or snacks that help to fulfill the obligations of the plan, and then slowly make the change.

- It can be very challenging to "give up" your old ways of eating. When you are really sure that you are depriving yourself of favorite foods, it is quite likely that you will return to eating them whenever an emotional challenge is presented. Don't allow yourself to feel deprived by simply making a gradual shift into DASH eating.

- You need to really master the DASH way of eating before you can easily head out to a restaurant or enjoy a road trip that involves meals on the go. When you tackle the day to day eating first and then attempt to use DASH while dining out, you are going to enjoy success and feel much better about the entire issue.

- Beginning to diet and exercise all at once, and to a degree that some might find challenging, can make you feel unwell. Instead, use some time to track eating and exercise (as already recommended) and then make some gradual changes that become a "habit" rather than a temporary change. In other words, don't make the DASH diet plan a sort of destination. If you see it as something with an "end in sight" it means you are looking at it the wrong way. Rather, look at it as making positive and permanent changes in your life, and changes that have to become regular habits.

Don't sabotage your chances for success by jumping in over your head. Instead, really start to master what it means to use DASH eating plans and recipes. Below are five tips that we have seen put to use to get people off to a great start, get them back on track, and keep them moving forward with their plans.

TOP FIVE TIPS FOR A GOOD START TO DASH

You also have to remember one major thing about DASH dieting (and any dieting really) and that is that you will slip up, go off track, eat things you shouldn't, sit on the couch all weekend, etc.

Instead of allowing this to entirely derail your excellent goals and intention, use the following five tips for getting (and keeping) a good start:

1. Gather together some DASH specific recipes. Use these to begin slowly incorporating DASH-type meals into your daily life. If you do this for two short weeks you are going to find it very easy to begin eating all of your meals around such patterns.

2. When something works, write it down and do it again. For instance, if you really enjoyed a recipe you have to be sure that you use it as one of your "go to" resources. Just like the salty macaroni and cheese dish that you used to use as a last minute dinner solution, that stir fry recipe you enjoyed for lunch can easily become the new "go to". The same applies for snacks and other meal options.

3. Accept the slip and move on. Something that a lot of people do is allow themselves to head totally off track because of one small slip. This is no reason to "trash" the entire DASH diet plan and give up. Instead, just accept that it happened, ask yourself why, and then move on.

4. Create a checklist. Use the list of 11 items above to create your own checklist, and then break down the transition into DASH into small steps. For example, don't cram all of the "must do" items on the list into a single week. Instead, why not meet with your doctor and discuss the matter, do some research about whole food grocery stores on another day, and clean the pantry yet another? If you do this in steps it will be manageable and not overwhelming or daunting.

5. Always choose "actionable" goals. If you are vague about the reasons or the ways you will begin to use DASH, you are going to set yourself up for failure. Instead, choose goals that are specific, achievable, measurable, relevant, and which have deadlines. Don't get this wrong, it can be something as amazingly simple as saying: "My goal is to eat only fruit on the weekdays and then to enjoy a cookie on each weekend day". That is something that is very specific, trackable, achievable, relevant to your overall plans, and which has a deadline.

Use these five tips to get started, or re-started if you had a slip, and you are sure to enjoy success.

TIPS FOR USING DASH WHEN DINING OUT

Your one big challenge when doing the DASH way of life will be when you go to a restaurant. These are places that are very guilty of feeding the human craving for salty foods. These are also the places that will usually fill you with twice as many calories as you had planned to eat.

So, consider the following tips to help you avoid trouble when you dine out while following DASH:

1. Focus on what you CAN have, rather than what you cannot have. This allows you to enjoy the experience and still stick to your plans. For example, you won't be able to get the jumbo basket of fries and the enormous cheeseburger, but you can have the special of the day that features steamed fish, a huge green salad, roasted seasonal vegetables, and some whole grain pasta.

2. Ask how the foods are prepared. For example, most professional servers are totally fine with a patron asking about MSG, salt, sodium, and other ingredients. In fact, many restaurants are prepared for such questions and are happy to give full answers upon request.

3. Take the salt shaker and set it on the neighboring table, or out of your reach.

4. Ask that condiments like pickles, ketchup, mustard, sauces, and any other sodium-rich ingredients be kept off of your plate. This includes salad dressings, which can be easily replaced with a splash of oil and a squeeze of citrus or a small dash of vinegar.

5. Always ask to swap out the sodium heavy side dishes with simpler choices. Steamed vegetables, fresh fruit cups, and other whole foods are often able to replace those that you should not ingest.

6. Be aware of the sodium levels of the "freebies" in many restaurants too. Chips and dip, peanuts in the shell, breadsticks and crackers...these are loaded with sodium and to be avoided. Yes, even the bread and butter! Get used to bringing something from home if this is going to be a problem for you. Anything from carrot sticks to a bag of grapes can be easily carried and discreetly consumed at the table.

TIPS FOR USING DASH WHEN SHOPPING AND COOKING

We have already recommended that you become a perimeter shopper to the greatest extent possible because that helps you to avoid buying those jars of sauce, packaged meals, and other foods that are literally saturated with sodium.

What can you purchase on the perimeter? Use this recommended DASH shopping list to help you stock your shelves and make the DASH lifestyle easier to follow. There are some canned and pre-made foods in the list, but note that all are marked as "low sodium", "fat free", etc.

DASH Shopping List

Vegetables:

- Artichokes
- Asparagus
- Avocados
- Beets

- Bell peppers
- Broccoli
- Brussels sprouts
- Cabbage
- Carrots
- Cauliflower
- Celery
- Corn
- Cucumbers
- Eggplant
- Green beans
- Leafy greens
- Leeks
- Mushrooms
- Onions
- Peas
- Potatoes
- Radishes
- Root vegetables
- Spinach
- Squash
- Tomatoes

Fruits:

- Apples
- Apricots
- Bananas
- Berries
- Cherries
- Oranges
- Dates
- Figs
- Grapefruit
- Grapes
- Kiwi
- Lemons
- Limes
- Mango
- Melons
- Peaches
- Papaya
- Pears
- Pineapple
- Plums
- Prunes

Protein Sources:

- Beef
- Chicken (skinless)
- Eggs
- Pork tenderloin
- Salmon
- Shrimp
- Tempeh
- Tofu
- Turkey (skinless)

Grains:

- Barley
- Bran Cereal
- Brown rice
- Bulgur
- Couscous (whole wheat)
- Kasha (buckwheat)
- Low fat granola
- Muesli
- Pasta (Whole Wheat or Brown Rice)
- Quinoa, Millet, Amaranth
- Spelt, Triticale, Kamut
- Steel Cut Oats

- Whole Grain Cereal
- Wild rice

Dairy:

- Buttermilk (low fat)
- Cheese
- Cottage cheese (low fat)
- Kefir
- Margarine
- Milk (low fat)
- Sour cream (low fat)
- Yogurt (low fat)

Nuts and Seeds:

- Almonds
- Cashews
- Hazelnuts
- Nut butter
- Peanuts
- Pecans
- Seeds
- Soy nuts
- Walnut

Accepted Canned Goods:

- Applesauce (unsweetened)
- Beans and lentils
- Broth (low sodium)
- Chiles (diced)
- Chili sauce or hot sauce (low sodium)
- Fresh salsa or Pico de gallo (low sodium)
- Fruit-only or low-sugar spreads
- Hummus (low sodium)
- Marinara sauce (low sodium)
- Mayonnaise (low-fat)
- Mustard (low sodium)
- Oil: canola, olive, sesame
- Pesto (low sodium)
- Salad dressing (low fat)
- Salmon or tuna (in water)
- Soup (low sodium)
- Soy sauce (low sodium)
- Sun-dried tomatoes
- Tomato paste (low sodium)
- Tomato sauce (low sodium)
- Tomatoes (low sodium)
- Vinegar

Helpful Extras:

- Herbs (dried and fresh)

- Spices of all kinds (skip any blends that use sodium or MSG)

- Popcorn to be used in an air popper

- Dried fruits

- Herbal tea

- Sodium-free vegetable juices

- No sugar fruit juices (be sure they are 100%)

- Sparkling water (a reasonable alternative to soda)

How to Read Labels

We have mentioned becoming a good label reader several times. We haven't, however, gone over what it is you must look for as you read through the labels. By now, you probably have guessed that the first thing to look at is sodium, but that is actually a bit off the mark. What you need to first consider is the serving size in the package or the can.

Why? All of the nutrient information is going to be based on that serving size. Not only does knowing how much of each package qualifies as a single serving useful in terms of planning your diet, but it also allows you to gauge whether or not a food is worth eating. For example, if a small can of beans contains more than 25% of your daily sodium, and the can is the serving size, you may not want to use it.

Remember too that any serving size is subjective, and what we eat may not actually be the recommended serving size. You may opt for a much larger "serving" or even a smaller one, and that offsets the anticipated nutrients, calories, sodium, and fat.

So, first determine an actual serving size and then checkout that sodium.

All labels have to have sodium indicated per serving size and in milligrams per serving. The labels also tell you what percentage of your daily diet the amount of sodium represents. Any food that has 5% of less of the daily value of sodium is immediately to be considered a low sodium choice. If the label shows that a food has 20% or more of the recommended sodium amount it is a high sodium food, and probably best if avoided.

What else should you know about labels? The ingredients are usually in order of greatest to least quantity. This means that if you see sodium or any sort of sodium type of compound in the first few words of the ingredients it is probably a higher sodium food.

You can then apply the details taken from a label to your daily DASH plan to understand how it fits into the equation. For instance, if you choose a can of low sodium soup as a quick lunch, you need to also check the fat it contains, double check that it is indeed a low sodium food, and find out how many servings are in the can to be sure you don't overdo it when you eat it as the main component of a meal.

Using the Numbers from Labels and Food Lists

You will find the information on food labels, and even on food lists that give average calorie and nutrient counts for whole foods like fruit or meat, very useful. This is because you are going to want to monitor your diet according to your written plans and be sure that everything is adding up correctly.

Remember that the daily amounts for DASH are:

- Total fat: 27% of calories
- Saturated fat: 6% of calories
- Protein: 18% of calories
- Carbohydrate: 55% of calories
- Fiber: 30 g
- Cholesterol: 150 mg
- Sodium: 1,500 to 2,300 mg
- Potassium: 4,700 mg
- Calcium: 1,250 mg
- Magnesium: 500 mg

That means you need to do a bit of math if you want to know how many of your daily calories can be comprised of the nutrients. Don't worry...we've done the math for you and provided it below.

1,600 Calorie Diets

- Total Fat: 432 of your calories can come from fat.

- Total Saturated Fat: Only 96 of those fat calories can be of the saturated kind.

- Total Carbohydrates: 880 of your daily calories can come from carbs.

- Total Protein: 288 calories should come from protein.

2,000 Calorie Diets

- Total Fat: 540 of your calories can come from fat.

- Total Saturated Fat: Only 120 of those fat calories can be of the saturated kind.

- Total Carbohydrates: 1100 of your daily calories can come from carbs.

- Total Protein: 360 calories should come from protein.

2,600 Calorie Diets

- Total Fat: 702 of your calories can come from fat.

- Total Saturated Fat: Only 156 of those fat calories can be of the saturated kind.

- Total Carbohydrates: 1430 of your daily calories can come from carbs.

- Total Protein: 468 calories should come from protein.

With all of these figures and facts you are probably more than ready to begin planning your own DASH diet. The last chapter of Resources has the blank planners that you can use to begin tracking the way that you eat now, and then use them to develop your plans for starting to eat according to the DASH diet as well.

DASH RESOURCES & PLANNERS

To use the following planners/trackers requires some knowledge about portion equivalents.

Portions for DASH

Use the list below to help you with your tracking:

- Fruits: 1/2 cup portions. This is the same as 1/4 cup dried fruit, 1 medium fresh fruit, 1/2 cup frozen or fresh, and 4 ounces of pure juice.

- Vegetables: 1/2 cup portions. This is the same as 1 cup of greens, 1/2 cup fresh or frozen, 4 ounces of vegetable juice, and 1/2 cup rinsed canned vegetables.

- Dairy: one cup portions. This is the same as 8 ounces of milk or yogurt and 1.5 ounces of cheese.

- Grains: one ounce portions. This is the same as a single slice of bread, 1/2 cup cooked rice or pasta, and 1/2 of dried cereals.

- Meats: one ounce servings. This is the same as a single egg or an ounce of cooked meat, poultry or fish.

- Nuts, Seeds, or Legumes: portions vary and include 1/2 cooked beans or peas, 1/2 ounce of seeds, 2 tablespoons of peanut butter, and 1.5 ounces of fresh nuts.

- Oils: portions vary but include 1 teaspoon of margarine or vegetable oil, 1 tablespoon of low fat mayonnaise, and 2 tablespoons of light salad dressing.

- Sweets/Salt/Alcohol - used vary sparingly, this would include 1 tablespoon of jam, 1 cup of lemonade, 1/2 sorbet, etc.

You can use these serving sizes as you develop or track daily food intake.

DASH Planners

Use the following blank planners to note the foods, and the amounts eaten at each meal. For example, a whole wheat bagel with two tablespoons of peanut butter would be tracked as 2 oz. of whole Grains (or whatever weight the bagel was) and a single portion of Nuts, Seeds, or Beans.

DASH Day Planner - 1600 Calories

Total Daily Recommended Amounts:

- Fruit: 2 Cups
- Vegetable: 1.5 to 2 Cups
- Low fat or fat free dairy: 2-3 Cups
- Grains: 6 ounces
- Lean meats: 3-6 ounces
- Nuts, Seeds, or Beans: 4-5 times weekly
- Oil: 2 teaspoons
- Sweets/Salt/Alcohol

Breakfast:

- Fruit
- Vegetable
- Low fat or fat free dairy
- Grains
- Lean meats
- Nuts, Seeds, or Beans
- Oil
- Sweets/Salt/Alcohol

Lunch:

- Fruit

- Vegetable

- Low fat or fat free dairy

- Grains

- Lean meats

- Nuts, Seeds, or Beans

- Oil

- Sweets/Salt/Alcohol

Dinner:

- Fruit

- Vegetable

- Low fat or fat free dairy

- Grains

- Lean meats

- Nuts, Seeds, or Beans

- Oil

- Sweets/Salt/Alcohol

Snacks:

- Fruit

- Vegetable

- Low fat or fat free dairy

- Grains

- Lean meats

- Nuts, Seeds, or Beans

- Oil

- Sweets/Salt/Alcohol

TOTALS

DASH Day Planner - 2000 Calories

Total Daily Recommended Amounts:

- Fruit: 2-2.5 Cups

- Vegetable: 2-2.5 Cups

- Low fat or fat free dairy: 2-3 Cups

- Grains: 6-8 ounces

- Lean meats: 6 or less ounces

- Nuts, Seeds, or Beans: 4-5 times weekly

- Oil: 2-3 teaspoons

- Sweets/Salt/Alcohol

Breakfast:

- Fruit

- Vegetable

- Low fat or fat free dairy

- Grains

- Lean meats

- Nuts, Seeds, or Beans

- Oil

- Sweets/Salt/Alcohol

Lunch:

- Fruit

- Vegetable

- Low fat or fat free dairy

- Grains

- Lean meats

- Nuts, Seeds, or Beans

- Oil

- Sweets/Salt/Alcohol

Dinner:

- Fruit

- Vegetable

- Low fat or fat free dairy

- Grains

- Lean meats

- Nuts, Seeds, or Beans

- Oil

- Sweets/Salt/Alcohol

Snacks:

- Fruit

- Vegetable

- Low fat or fat free dairy

- Grains

- Lean meats

- Nuts, Seeds, or Beans

- Oil

- Sweets/Salt/Alcohol

TOTALS

DASH Day Planner - 2600 Calories

Total Daily Recommended Amounts:

- Fruit: 2.5-3 Cups

- Vegetable: 2.5-3 Cups

- Low fat or fat free dairy: 3 Cups

- Grains: 10-11 ounces

- Lean meats: 6 ounces

- Nuts, Seeds, or Beans: 1 portion per day

- Oil: 2-3 teaspoons

- Sweets/Salt/Alcohol

Breakfast:

- Fruit

- Vegetable

- Low fat or fat free dairy

- Grains

- Lean meats

- Nuts, Seeds, or Beans

- Oil

- Sweets/Salt/Alcohol

Lunch:

- Fruit
- Vegetable
- Low fat or fat free dairy
- Grains
- Lean meats
- Nuts, Seeds, or Beans
- Oil
- Sweets/Salt/Alcohol

Dinner:

- Fruit
- Vegetable
- Low fat or fat free dairy
- Grains
- Lean meats
- Nuts, Seeds, or Beans
- Oil
- Sweets/Salt/Alcohol

Snacks:

- Fruit

- Vegetable

- Low fat or fat free dairy

- Grains

- Lean meats

- Nuts, Seeds, or Beans

- Oil

- Sweets/Salt/Alcohol

TOTALS

CONCLUSION

You can now begin the DASH diet. We hope you find the resources useful and enjoy success with your plans. Whether you want to drop blood pressure a small amount, or even by up to 14 points, we are sure you can accomplish many good things using this plan.

Just be sure to keep track of your progress and use the planners to keep yourself on track and really master DASH eating.

Good luck and good health!

MORE BOOKS BY SUSAN ELLERBECK

Raw Food Diet For Beginners

Plant Based Diet For Beginners

Smoothie Recipes for Beginners

Juicing Recipes for Beginners

Vegetarian Recipes for Beginners

Vegan Recipes for Beginners

74449028R00053

Made in the USA
Middletown, DE
24 May 2018